HAIRY PIGSKINS
&
HIDDEN BLESSINGS

HAIRY PIGSKINS
&
HIDDEN BLESSINGS

Unexpected Places
Beyond the Comfort Zone

JEAN FLOYD

ISBN: 979-8-9934093-0-6
Front Cover Photo by David Floyd
Back Cover Photo by Jean Floyd
Cover and Interior Design by Eduardo Gonzalez Ripoll

TABLE OF CONTENTS

ACKNOWLEDGMENTS

To everyone who ever told me, "You should write a book," this book is for you. It took me years and years to stop laughing politely at you, followed by additional years to take you seriously. And then it required even more years to figure out when I would actually have time to write a book.

It turns out I had already written a book—to you. These stories were written to you and for you. I only needed the time to compile and refine them. This is my first offering to you of stories that have been written as devotions. Many other stories are yet to come.

Thanks to all who ever prayed for this process. I knew it would need many prayers—and it did. Your work of prayer has now come to fruition.

Thanks to all who ever read over a newsletter or story for me—mainly my dear husband (who had the dangerous and delicate balance of affirming while critiquing), my sisters, sometimes a brother-in-law, my dad, and occasionally my own children.

Thanks to my colleagues in Paraguay, who have lived this very fun life with me.

Thanks to all who believed that I could and should actually do this when I didn't believe it myself. You were God's voice to me.

Mainly, thanks to Jesus, my Good Shepherd, for guiding me through the whole process.

Introduction

When my husband, Tony, and I arrived in rural Paraguay in 1998, we came with a calling, a big yellow crate of worldly possessions, and hearts full of faith—but few concrete plans for church planting.

As we learned the language and adapted to the culture, God planted seeds of His church in a place where there had been no gospel witness. We also fixed appliances, taught English, repaired furniture, and raised three creative boys— homeschooling them from kindergarten through high school.

After fourteen years, we felt called to move further out, where there was once again no gospel witness.

Over the years, we've written many letters to friends, family, and supporters back home. This devotional is drawn from those letters—real moments of our missionary life captured in stories, spiritual reflections, and insights God whispered in the middle of dishes, diaper pins, piglets, and prayer walks. I offer you snippets of raising young kids on the mission field, planting a church, going on home assignments, doing evangelism and discipleship, and moving to another location to do it all again.

You don't have to live in Paraguay—or be a missionary—to find yourself in these pages. These devotional stories are about being human, being faithful, and being loved by a God who never leaves us, no matter where we are.

My hope is that you'll find quiet encouragement here.

That you'll laugh.

Maybe cry.

And maybe hear God speaking directly to you.

CHAPTER ONE

A Cherished Moment

I crouched on my haunches beside my friend, mimicking her posture. The winter day was warm, and we both peered into a little gathering of dead sticks underneath a small bush.

A mother pig nestled there with her seven newborn piglets, all in a row, where they had fallen asleep while nursing. A few of them were pink and shiny, just like the picture books. The others had mottled spots—some black and brown, some black and white.

We hunkered there exclaiming over them and chatting amiably. My friend was glad that her pig had finally given birth, and she had motioned for me to follow her across her dirt yard to show me where the new mother was.

"Do you like the pink ones or the spotted ones?" she asked.

"I like them all."

"I'll give you one when they are big enough," she said. "Do you want a male or female?"

"Oh, I don't really know. I love raising all kinds of animals, but I didn't grow up that way. This will be my first pig," I explained.

Then I told her a story of when my husband, Tony, and I first came to Paraguay. Someone sold me what I thought was a laying hen. I was so excited about having my own eggs. But when it started crowing, I realized it was a rooster. I wasn't going to get any eggs after all. That began my education about farm animals.

We both laughed. Then we got up from our hunkering vantage point and walked toward some trees hanging heavy with bright orange fruit.

"This one is bitter Seville oranges," she said. "They're rarely used for anything."

But the next tree had some smaller oranges.

"Let's pick some of these. They're sweet and good for juice," she said.

She went to get a bag for the fruit and a rake to reach into the tree and yank off the fruit. We poked and pulled and picked up the fruit when it fell—and we chatted as we did so.

This entire episode lasted only about ten minutes. Then I hurried home, across the dirt road, because some visitors had arrived at my house.

I hadn't shared the gospel with my friend (that's another story). We hadn't prayed. And I didn't quote any Bible verses.

But this was a cherished moment for me—one that I took a mental snapshot of to savor again and again. Something had passed between us that was warm and friendly and genuine. A relationship was forming, and this encounter with pigs and oranges was one block in the foundation.

Relationships build a platform of trust so that when the gospel is shared, it will stick. This is where church planting starts. If we live our lives intentionally, loving others deeply and letting our words and interactions be full of grace, then God has fertile ground to do His work.

- -

With whom will you share some everyday moments in order to build a relationship?

- -

Let your conversation be always full of grace,
seasoned with salt.

Colossians 4:6

CHAPTER TWO

The Catastrophic Cake

My teenage neighbor asked me to make a two-kilo cake for her and her classmates to celebrate the end of the school year.

The timing wasn't ideal. My family was packing for a trip to the city. I was in the middle of Christmas baking. We had a wedding to attend. It was summer in the Southern hemisphere. Firing up the stove for two hours when the temperatures were already in the upper 90s—inside my house—was an uncomfortable sacrifice.

A two-kilo cake is no small task. Two kilos doesn't mean the finished cake weighs two kilos—it means the recipe has two kilos of flour in it. That's about fifteen cups!

My neighbor brought all the ingredients to me mid-morning the day before our trip. I quickly made the batter, baked it for two hours, and set it out to cool. Then

I began the tedious task of layering: cake, peach juice, plenty of dulce de leche, sliced peaches, icing … then another layer of cake. The outside was piped with little icing stars—enough to cover the whole, enormous cake.

I was proud of myself for finishing it quickly and beautifully. One more task checked off the list.

Tony carried the cake to the neighbors' house since it weighed much more than two kilos after it was baked and decorated. We crossed the uneven cow field in the blazing sun when, to my horror, the top layers began to slide.

Slop!

A big glob of icing dropped like a strangely white cow pie on the dirt path.

When our neighbors heard our exclamations, they came out to meet us. We all hurried to a table on their porch with hands outspread around the cake like basketball players guarding the coveted ball.

Tony set the cake down just in time for us to watch it rift into pieces—like the earth opening up and shifting its tectonic plates. I caught one continent as it tried to slide onto the table. With my precious piped icing oozing between my fingers, I slid that continent back on top of the world only to watch another continent slip off the other edge.

My neighbor caught it and tried to slide it back on.

I have never had a more catastrophic cake experience.

What could I do but laugh as my neighbor and I scooped and slopped and patted the top layer of the cake back in place? My beautiful cake was a complete wreck—

certainly not fit for a table centerpiece at a graduation party.

Grasping for a shred of hope, my neighbor asked if I could make another layer for the top. I still had so much to do. I looked at her rather hopelessly but promised to do *something* before we left the next morning, and we put the catastrophic cake in her refrigerator.

True to Paraguayan wedding customs, we were out past midnight. But because we have a cow to milk, Tony and I were up early to get our sure-to-be-a-long-day started. After milking then pasteurizing, I made more icing. I took it down to the neighbors to patch up the pathetic cake.

As I piped delicate stars of icing over the mess that had been patted and patched together, I shared with them what I had been pondering.

The cake was meant to be something beautiful. So are our lives, but because of our sinful nature and life's jarring circumstances, they can become a mess.

We try to fix it ourselves—scooping, slopping, and patting our life back together to make some semblance of the right form. But the mess tends to ooze through our fingers, and we just make an uglier mess, not fit to be seen. Then we top it with a lovely layer of icing to make it seem fine.

But under the icing, the disaster is still there.

People who don't know us well may not see the mess, but God does. He came to earth as a human—to pay the debt of death we owe for our sins. Not just to cover up the yuckiness like we try to do but to completely take away the nasty mess so we can start over with a brand-new life. That's what 2 Corinthians 5:17 says: the old will be gone and we can be a whole new creation.

My cake needed a whole do-over, not just a cover-up. God offers us exactly that because of Jesus. So, while I'm not glad my cake was a disaster, I *am* grateful it gave me a chance to tell my neighbor how God can do more than patch us up—He can make us new.

I pray for more real-life opportunities like this. This is what friendship evangelism is—and where church planting begins.

. . . .

Have you ever tried to patch up your life with messy results?

Do you need a complete do-over?

Who might need this encouragement about messy lives?

. . . .

Therefore, if anyone is in Christ, the new creation has come: The old has gone, the new is here!

2 Corinthians 5:17

CHAPTER THREE

The Hairy Pigskin Factor

During our first few months in Paraguay, we were introduced to many traditional Paraguayan foods. On one special occasion, our host proudly presented us with something that looked fancy— but not super appealing.

It was some sort of cold meat and vegetable medley, rolled up and sliced like a sweet roll. The layers swirled in a dizzy pattern—something white, a thin layer of meat-like substance, some mixed vegetables—all spiraling onto the plate.

Our host proudly told me how it was made.

Take a pigskin, lay it out flat, then spread some chopped vegetables on it. Roll it up, tie it tightly with string, and boil it for a long time. Once it cools in the refrigerator, slice it and serve cold.

I inspected more closely what was on my plate, and I could see that some of the hair was left on the outside of the pigskin. I didn't know whether to hope that the thick, white layer was skin or fat—both equally unappealing.

Tony whispered quietly to me, "In the States this is what we make footballs out of—not food." My eyebrows went up slightly.

Why would people eat hairy pigskins when there are steaks and prime ribs in the world?

Too often our spiritual lives are like this.

We settle for something we don't even realize is disgusting. A man can't let go of his bitterness and drowns his sorrows in alcohol. He lives life from one stupor to another, rejecting the abundant life that is offered to him if only he will follow God.

Too many children are born out of wedlock, then raised by aging grandparents. Instead of choosing a secure, happy, monogamous relationship, the parents lead separate lives riddled with jealousy and bitterness. The parents miss out on the joy of watching their child grow up in a loving, whole home.

This is what I call the hairy pigskin factor.

Settling for something less than the best, less than what God wants to give.

It's settling for scraps when we are offered a feast—settling for the hairy pigskin instead of having steak or prime rib.

God has a myriad of delicacies available to us when we follow His will for our lives.

But too often we choose our own way.

What is your hairy pigskin?

Once you let go, you will most likely find that what you were holding on to was really tasteless, or even disgusting, compared to what God has to offer.

- -

What are you holding on to that you need to let go of?

- -

Come, all you who are thirsty, come to the waters, and you who have no money, come, buy and eat! Come, buy wine and milk without money and without cost. Why spend money on what is not bread, and your labor on what does not satisfy? Listen, listen to me, and eat what is good, and your soul will delight in the richest of fare.

Isaiah 55:1–3

CHAPTER FOUR

The Riches of Lettuce

W hen we first went to Paraguay, we missed iceberg lettuce. It was nonexistent there. The only option was the darker green leaf lettuce that we weren't accustomed to. We missed our crisp salads with a juicy crunch.

But slowly, as time passed, we learned that the dark green leaf lettuce actually had more flavor and was more satisfying. We found several varieties of it, even some red lettuce, and planted it in our garden. Before long, we truly preferred it over the former.

The iceberg lettuce had lost its appeal. It seemed watered down and tasteless compared to the deep vitamin-rich flavor of leaf lettuce. It seemed empty compared to what we presently enjoyed.

This is like our spiritual walk toward God.

At first, the things of the world seem to be the only option. We don't know there is more. The worldly things seem pleasing and good—and the words of God seem too strong.

But as we read more of God's Word and learn more about Him, we begin to discover the richer life He offers. Then the things of the world start to lose their appeal. Soon they seem tasteless—void of true nourishment. We now crave the deeper things that are so much more satisfying. Romans 11:33 talks about the incredible depth and richness of knowing God. How nourishing!

This realization gives me hope as a steward of God's Word.

We ourselves are not responsible for changing people's lives. We don't need to tell them what they do or don't have to do. We don't have to force change or dictate rules. We just expose them to the gospel and to God's Word.

The Holy Spirit does His job to give them a taste for Him.

Gradually they will find that the things they were doing and the places where they were looking for happiness have lost their appeal. The way they were dressing, the things they were saying, the situations they turned to for meaning—they will all lose their flavor.

And they will naturally hunger for the deeper things of God.

- -

What is your iceberg lettuce that now tastes bland?

Who needs to be exposed to the gospel so they will hunger for deeper things?

- -

Oh, the depth of the riches both of the wisdom and knowledge of God! How unsearchable are His judgments and unfathomable His ways!

Romans 11:33

CHAPTER FIVE

Rest

Naptime had finally arrived. I was glad my three-year-old son was sleeping. He looked so relaxed. His bare feet, dirty from all the running, were resting on the crisp white sheets, and his breaths were long and slow. His long, thick eyelashes were nestled against his tan cheeks. He'd been playing hard that day, and he was a bit sick too. He needed the rest. I was happy his body could be refreshed and ready to go again so I could watch his merry antics that always brought a smile to my face.

My eight-month-old son was finally sleeping too. His body was curled up cozily. His chubby cherub cheeks perfectly framed his tender parted lips. His breaths were as gentle as a feather drifting softly through the air. I was glad he was resting. He had worked hard that day. He had recently learned to pull up and to sit up, so he had been practicing both nonstop. He was about to take off crawling too. He so often fought sleep even though he was tired. He needed the rest so he could continue growing, learning, and playing. It made me happy to see him sleep.

I wonder if that is how God feels about us when we rest. I'm sure that we please God just as much when we are resting—when that is His will for us—as when we are hard at work for Him. But how we fight it, don't we? We tend to think that rest is lazy. But just like I know when my children need rest and am pleased when they do, God knows when we need it too—and delights when we finally give in.

Our family had recently enjoyed a much-needed rest. We had a wonderful two weeks away from home. We spent the first week at a hotel nestled in an uncharacteristically beautiful jungle-like atmosphere about three hours south of us in Paraguay. We made family memories swimming in the pool, walking in the woods, and playing Go Fish or watching DVDs together. The second week, another missionary family joined us with their two young boys, and we went to Brazil, about four hours away. There we rode go-carts, went fishing, visited a water park, and played at lots of restaurant playgrounds. What fun times we had.

Deuteronomy says that the one the Lord loves rests between His shoulders—like a child sleeping on his father's chest. That is delightful for both father and child. I think God was as glad as we were for the opportunity for us to get away and be refreshed and for the family memories we made.

- -

Are you discerning when God tells you to rest,
or do you fight it?

How does He see you when you are resting?

Can you imagine Him delighting in your rest,
just as you might delight in a sleeping child or
baby?

- -

*Let the beloved of the L*ORD *rest secure in Him,*
for He shields Him all day long, and the one
*the L*ORD *loves rests between His shoulders.*

Deuteronomy 33:12

CHAPTER SIX

A Worshiping Parent

Have you ever thought of worshiping God through the enjoyment of parenting? The Westminster Catechism says, "The chief end of man is to glorify God and enjoy Him forever."

We are created to worship God. And we can worship Him through our everyday acts. Romans 12:1 says that true worship is offering up our whole lives, our very being, to Him. That includes diapers, lost shoes, and late-night feedings. I worship Him by being the best parent I can be. I worship Him by serving my family. I worship Him through my menial tasks.

I worship Him not just *while* I change a dirty diaper but *by* changing a dirty diaper. I am doing what I was created to do—and that is worship.

I worship God by cooking a meal.

I worship God by folding pajamas.

I worship God by rescuing a lost toy from behind the bed and putting it back in its place.

I worship God by posting a scribbled picture on the refrigerator and reminding myself of the profundity of little fingers able to do that.

I worship God by taking time out to swing my kids.

I worship God by putting shoes on my children's feet.

I worship God by feeding a baby at 3:00 a.m.

I worship God by tying a cape onto a superhero.

I worship God by *enjoying* all these things instead of doing them with drudgery.

In doing these, I am fulfilling my purpose, and that is worship.

Have you ever felt your heart bursting at the seams as you feel the soft, warm, squishy weight of your baby as his body relaxes, melting into yours, as he falls asleep in your arms, his cherub face resting against your chest, drool dripping like honey from his parted lips?

Have you felt like dancing when you see your four-year-old son's whole face light up with a smile that makes his eyes sparkle like diamonds set in luscious, long, gold-filigree eyelashes? Have you felt like singing when you hear your two-year-old's infectious giggle that spills out of his toothy grin when you press your face into his tummy? Have you noticed the gentle sound of your baby sucking his fingers, his sleepy, blinking eyes carefully studying your face as you cuddle him?

Notice. Laugh. Sing. Dance. Enjoy. Savor. And love those moments. Hold them up to God as praise, worshiping Him for His marvelous works. Praise Him that you have these moments to relish as a parent—to delight in worshiping Him by enjoying being what He created you to be.

- -

Which everyday tasks do you see as chores?

How could viewing them as worship transform you?

- -

Offer your bodies as a living sacrifice, holy and pleasing to God—this is your true and proper worship.

Romans 12:1

CHAPTER SEVEN

For Lack of Connectors

"Where is that PCMCIA card?" Tony asked as we pulled various things from our travel-weary bags.

"I have no idea what that is," I answered.

"It lets us do email," Tony clarified.

There were some frustrations with getting settled again in Paraguay after home assignment—and with life in general. For lack of a small part or tool that connects two things together, entire plans can often grind to a halt. Our current frustrations involved two such missing connectors.

The first was this adapter that connected our cell phone to our computer so that we could send and receive emails. We kept thinking it would turn up as we unpacked and settled in, but it hadn't yet. We had the phone, and we had the computer, but they couldn't communicate without the connector. So, for the time being we were back to our former ways—driving one to two hours to a colleague's house to check email.

The second connector we lacked was diaper pins. We unpacked the antiquated rectangular cloth diapers and the plastic diaper covers from storage and reluctantly started to use them, only to find that the diaper pins that hold those white rectangles together around a squirmy baby were not with them. Such a small item, but without it, the whole process is disabled.

This is typical of life in Paraguay. The clinic in our town showed us that they had IV bags and tubes—but no needles to insert the IV. They had needles for putting in stitches—but no thread. Beds for patients to stay overnight—but no sheets. In other places, we saw badly needed road equipment sitting beside the road idle because there was no gasoline.

We also see this same lack of connectors spiritually in Paraguay. Almost everyone knows about the Bible, and there is plenty of religious interest. But the Connector—Jesus—the One who links our Almighty Creator with man's heart, is not understood. People may have all the right components, but they haven't *clicked* because they don't know Jesus. Such a simple but vital link is missing. First Timothy 2:5 confirms that Jesus is the only connector that will work. "For there is one God and one mediator between God and mankind, the man Christ Jesus."

When Tony and I feel the frustration with our lack of physical connectors, we are reminded that God called us here to bring this much more important spiritual

Connector to the people of Paraguay. We pray for great understanding to click in people's hearts as we tell them about Jesus, their connection to eternity.

. . . .

Whom do you need to connect to Jesus?

How would you describe your own connection with Jesus?

Is anything missing?

. . . .

For there is one God and one mediator
between God and mankind, the man
Christ Jesus

1 Timothy 2:5

CHAPTER 8

Window to Our World

Making a to-do list makes me think about what Nancy Leigh DeMoss says in her book *Lies Women Believe*. The number one lie women identified with was "I don't have time to do everything I'm supposed to do." Can you relate? Probably, especially around any holiday.

Our family was looking forward to a big Thanksgiving day celebration with our larger mission family. Here is a to-do list that will give you a window into our world. Of course, every day is different, and the next list may contain very different types of activities—but for what it's worth, here's one list I made:

- Write newsletter.
- Write Thanksgiving email to those coming to our house to let them know who is bringing what.

- Pick beans.
- Can beans.
- Shear sheep.
- Wash old sheepskin.
- Plant flowers.
- Clean off jelly hutch.
- Cut hair. (ALL my boys!)
- Replant banana trees. (They need spreading out because lots of new ones come up around the old ones.)
- Kill turkey.

Tony's List:
- Fix guitar for a guy. (The body got smashed.)
- Repair plumbing at our colleagues' house. (They haven't had hot water in their kitchen sink for months, and recently even the cold water was leaking like crazy.)
- Prune plants and otherwise get the yard ready for visitors.
- Get ready for big meeting on Friday after Thanksgiving.

In Nancy's book, she reminds us that Jesus Himself only had thirty-three years to complete His work. But when He finished, He said, "I have brought you glory on earth by completing *the work you gave me to do*" (emphasis added). He didn't get everything done that His disciples or other people wanted Him to do. But He did do everything *His Father* wanted Him to do.

The truth is that all we have to do is what *God* assigns to us, and there *is* time to do everything on *His* to-do list for us. Our frustrations come when we try to do things that are not on *His* list. Nancy says:

> When I establish my own agenda or let others determine the priorities for my life, rather than taking time to discern what it is that God wants me to do, I end up buried … with guilt, frustration, and haste, rather than enjoying the peaceful, well-ordered life that He intends.★

May you rightly discern all that the *Father* wants you to do as you enter this day, week, or season—so you can enjoy a peaceful, ordered, haste-free holiday or *holy* day.

P. S. I didn't get everything on the list done, but that's OK.

★Nancy Leigh Demoss, *Lies Women Believe and the Truth That Sets Them Free*, Chicago: Moody Press, 2001, 119.

- -

What is on your to-do list versus God's to-do list for you?

- -

I have brought you glory on earth by finishing the work you gave me to do.

John 17:4

CHAPTER NINE

What is Church?

"**M**ommy, are we going to church?" my five-year-old asked one Sunday as we were walking along a dusty trail beside a cotton field.

We had left our car behind when it couldn't go any further on the deeply rutted road, and we walked the kilometer or so to the small wooden house where a family was waiting for us to read the Bible with them.

"Yes," I told my son, "but it's not like the church in the States."

On Sunday mornings I often pondered the Church—the Body of Christ. It is so diverse and beautiful. The church we were walking to continued strong for many years, even though later we only went every other week to visit them on Sunday afternoons. That family still loved God and enjoyed reading His Word together.

Later, on Sunday mornings, we went to church in our own backyard. Our friends gathered in a circle, sitting in a variety of plastic or wooden chairs. Usually, the white slatted porch swing—hung between two big trees—was part of the circle and chock-full of wiggly kids. The dappled light coming through the leaves created a rural stained-glass on the dusty ground, dotted also with patches of struggling grass. The singing birds added background music, and the warm breeze whispered God's love.

As we sang praises to God and worshiped Him through our prayers, I thought of other parts of the Church and how beautiful they are too, like Paul talks about in 1 Corinthians chapter twelve.

The people in a vaulted ceiling cathedral in New York with a huge pipe organ making ethereal music that dances with the snowflakes swirling outside the stained-glass windows.

The people in California sitting around tables sipping coffee while discussing a Bible passage.

The people in South Carolina sitting on padded pews praising God through deeply meaningful, traditional hymns.

The people in Oklahoma praising God by painting pictures while listening to worship music and watching the dancers wave banners and flags.

The people in Africa praising God with harmonious acapella music and rhythm as deep as their heritage.

The people in Mongolia bundled in warm clothes inside a round yurt.

The people in China hiding in a cave at night to praise God.

They are all different. And all beautiful parts of the Church—the Body of Christ. God has made each one just as He wants them to be says 1 Corinthians 12:18.

Those who go.
Those who give.
Those who pray.
Those who are growing.
Those who are struggling.
Those who mourn.
Those who celebrate.
Those who teach.
Those who listen.
Those who are rich.
Those who are poor.

Each one is a beautiful part of the Church.

One particular evening, we gathered with another part of the Church in our friend's dusty yard. As the children played and giggled in front of the house, we sat with the adults on the side and retold a part of the Bible and discussed it as chicks, ducks, and the occasional pig wandered in and out of our relaxed gathering. God's presence was so real in this setting—as permeating as that beautiful organ music in the vaulted cathedral.

I wish that you could experience the thrill of hearing my friend spontaneously retell a Bible story with astonishing accuracy, her face lit with gentle joy as she talked and talked. I wish you could see firsthand how each life in that small circle was being transformed by God's Word. We love the Body of Christ, and we are especially fond of this part God gave us the privilege of nurturing.

Be encouraged today to remember that you are a part of something big, diverse, and very beautiful! I can't wait for the day when all the parts of the Body will meet one another and praise God together in beautiful, unified diversity!

- -

What is church to you?

What part do you play in the Body of Christ?

- -

But in fact God has placed the parts in the body, every one of them, just as He wanted them to be.

1 Corinthians 12:18

CHAPTER TEN

God Reads Newsletters

D id you know that God reads newsletters before they are sent out?

I discovered this one day as I was preparing to send a newsletter to the printer. I was expecting some final comments from my sister, who edits for me. I planned to make those last changes and send the newsletter on to the printer. But when I checked my email, a message from a supporting church caught my attention. The subject line was "Furlough." I knew I had mentioned in the newsletter that we would soon be on furlough and looking for a house and a car, but I didn't think anyone knew the dates yet. *Did I already send out the newsletter? Did they already read it?*

The email said the church was anticipating our upcoming furlough and wanted to know if we would like them to find a car for us to use during our time in the States. Wow. And that wasn't all. Unbeknownst to me at the moment—in that same batch of emails—before the newsletter had gone out—was *another* message from another church also asking about our furlough dates to ensure that their mission house would be available for us.

Double wow.

No, I hadn't already sent out the newsletter. But God knew our needs before we asked. Isaiah 65:24 says, "*Before they call I will answer; while they are still speaking, I will hear.*"

What a mighty God we serve!

So along with some other slight changes from my editor, I took out the part about needing a house and car before sending the newsletter to the printer. Be encouraged that God knows your needs before you even ask!

- -

When have you seen God answer before you
even asked?

Where do you still need to trust that God
hears you while you are speaking?

- -

*Before they call I will answer; while they are
still speaking, I will hear.*

Isaiah 65:24

CHAPTER ELEVEN

Grandparents

One month, we enjoyed a visit from my dad and his new wife, whom God so graciously brought into his life several years after my mom died. His new wife had been a missionary in Nigeria for many years with her late husband and five children.

Our boys basked in the time spent with grandparents, especially getting to know their new Gramma. They read books and played with toys together. They enjoyed just having their grandparents at the breakfast table, in the house, in the yard—in their lives for a while.

I wonder if God might feel toward us a bit like my boys feel about their grandparents. My boys didn't care if their grandparents came down here to *do* big projects—they just wanted to *be* with them. And they wanted their grandparents to enjoy being with them and to delight in them.

God is like this.

It doesn't matter so much what we *do* for Him. He mainly wants us to *be* with Him, rest in Him, and enjoy Him. Zephaniah 3:17 says that He takes great delight in us and even rejoices over us with singing. He basks in our delight in Him. And then it becomes reciprocal—we bask in His delight in us.

The grandparents did finish a few projects that month, but mostly we just basked and delighted in being together.

Time with grandparents is much too short. But thankfully, getting to know God and developing our relationship with Him is never-ending—so the basking and delighting keep on going!

. . . .

What needs to happen for you to bask in God's presence and His delight in you?

. . . .

The Lord *your God is with you. … He will take great delight in you … [He] will rejoice over you with singing.*

Zephaniah 3:17

CHAPTER TWELVE

Cleaning Windows

One day I was cleaning windows. We were living in a beautifully furnished mission house that was generously loaned to us for our year in the States. Since the place is generally occupied for only short stays by missionaries traveling through, the windows had been sorely neglected.

What a different perspective clean windows give a house! Looking through dingy, spider-webby windows doesn't make my heart soar. It makes me feel sluggish and dirty. It tends to make life seem mundane or even depressing. But seeing beautiful sunlight pouring through a totally transparent pane makes me want to smile. It lifts my heart and gives a bounce to my step. It makes me ready to face the day.

As I tediously cleaned the windows, I pondered how my spiritual life is like those windows. When I ignore my relationship with the Son because I am always on the go, my spiritual life becomes dingy and spider-webby. Not all at once. It is a slow fade—ignoring that relationship one day, then the next, then the next—until life feels gray and dim.

When I started cleaning a dingy window, the first swipes of that cloth made a huge difference. They revealed just how long it had been since the dirt had been dealt with. Light poured through the window with new vigor. Seeing such a difference made me want to keep going.

The same is true of my first steps back toward God. When I reach out to Him, He meets me right in the middle of my muck. He is so humble and gracious to vigorously shine new hope into my life even when I have ignored Him for so long.

I noticed something else about cleaning windows. The more I cleaned, the more I noticed the small smudges. It was painstaking work to get all the splotches and streaks off and the residual lint out of the corners.

Similarly in my spiritual life, the more I walk with God, the more He reveals the smudges and splotches. Sometimes a spot looks clean from one angle, but from another—especially when the light hits—it stands out clearly. It is hard to deal with that again—and feels like more work than the first swipe that opens up floods of light. But by then I am so gloriously into cleaning that I can't be satisfied until my life is totally transparent, letting

God shine His light through me to the world. I don't want anything to mar that. So, I keep working, letting Him reveal the smudges to me.

It was tempting to try to clean all the windows in the house at once. Once I noticed the dinginess, I wanted it all gone in one mad cleaning frenzy. But that would have been more than I could handle in one day—and would have exhausted me. So, I resolved to clean only one window at a time. Each time I cleaned one, it made me feel so good, and my house was filled with more light.

Spiritually, it takes patience to get cleaned up too. Instead of one mad cleaning frenzy, I can methodically deal with one issue at a time, which is more realistic. Second Corinthians 3:18 says that we are slowly transformed into His image as we contemplate His glory.

I looked forward to the day when I would be done with all the windows. In reality, though, I knew that once I finished, some would have already gotten dirty again. But if I kept at it constantly, they wouldn't be as dirty as they were the first time around, and a quick wipe might be all that was needed.

Spiritually I look forward to the day that my life lets God's light shine through un-smudged. On this earth, there are going to be things that hinder my relationship with Him. But if I have constant interaction with Him, I can keep the big grunge from building up and can quickly wipe away any uncleanness He reveals. So, I will work constantly and methodically, letting His light shine through me to give renewed hope and a bounce to my step.

. . . .

What keeps God's light from shining through you?

What spiritual windows do you need to clean in your life?

. . . .

But we all, with unveiled face, beholding as in a mirror the glory of the Lord, are being transformed into the same image from glory to glory, just as from the Lord, the Spirit.

2 Corinthians 3:18 (NASB95)

CHAPTER THIRTEEN

Two O'Clock— Rapturous Reunion

K nowing my youngest son when he was five years old was a delightful experience. His thin, blond hair bounced with his movements—which were ample and always done with beautiful, childish abandon. And his eyes. His eyes were marvelous half circles that were beacons of pure light when he smiled. He was the epitome of a bouncy, yellow smiley face.

Two o'clock was one of my favorite times of the day that year when we were in the States again on home assignment. That was the moment I was rapturously reunited with him—my kindergartener. As the hour approached, wherever I was, I smiled as I thought of the expression that would spread across his face when he saw me coming to pick him up.

Invariably, the moment he spotted me as I came to be reunited with him, his face lit up with utter glee beyond the sweetest delicacy imaginable. Then a smile spread across his face that could transform even the most sinister heart. My heart melted all over again when I saw his smile, and I couldn't wait to have him in my presence and share tales of our time apart.

Usually, we went home, and the school backpack was flung carelessly by the door. He bounced joyfully to the couch and eagerly told me about his day. Then we snuggled—enthralled with each other's presence—as I read him a story or two. These were some of the most precious moments of my day. My son delighted in me, and I delighted in him.

My heavenly Father also delights in time spent with me. He waits eagerly, scanning the crowd for my approach. When He spots me coming, His face lights up with delight that we will be reunited. He anticipates a beautiful time together, sharing from our hearts. He is utterly delighted that I have come to Him again—even if it is just to tell how my day has gone up until then. Zephaniah 3:17 tells us that He even rejoices over us with singing.

Am I as equally delighted with the thought of being reunited and spending time with my Father? Do I think of Him throughout the day eagerly awaiting our time together? Does my heart melt when I see His face? Do I fling the day's worries aside with careless abandon at the thought of snuggling at His side to listen to Him? Am I enthralled by His presence, and do I count our time together as the most precious moments of my day just like the psalmist, who only wanted one thing—to gaze on the beauty of the Lord? (Psalm 27:4)

When I glimpse the light that radiates from His face when He sees me coming from afar and sense His rapturous delight at our time together, how can my response be anything but yes, yes, yes—and yes!

- -

Can you imagine God eagerly awaiting to spend time with you?

Will you fling your worries aside and sit on His lap as you talk to each other?

- -

One thing I ask from the LORD, this only do I seek: that I may dwell in the house of the LORD all the days of my life, to gaze on the beauty of the LORD and to seek him in his temple.

Psalm 27:4

CHAPTER FOURTEEN

Our Best Clothes/Filthy Rags

Our standards define how we look at things around us. When we were in Paraguay packing our things to come to the States, I looked at our clothes to decide what would go with us to the States. With new standards in mind, I looked at them through different eyes. What was perfectly fine for Paraguay didn't hold up to American standards.

In Paraguay, clothing is totally utilitarian. Ripped, frayed, patched, stained—it doesn't matter. It puts something on your body that you can call clothing. Whether it matches or not is of no consequence.

So, when I got out our best clothes in Paraguay to bring them to the States, I started comparing them to a different standard. "Wow," I reflected, "I thought this one was really nice, but here are a few stains I never noticed—

that will never do." Or "look at this one—it's all frayed around the sleeves. I never noticed that before." And "my goodness, the boys' favorite shirts are full of little holes."

A verse in Isaiah comes vividly to mind. Isaiah 64:6 says, "All our righteous acts are like filthy rags." When we look at our good deeds compared to the world's standards, we think we have done well. "I must be a pretty good person," I muse. "Just look how nice I was. Surely God will be pleased with me." Or "surely my good will outweigh the bad, and God will let me into heaven." Just like those clothes in Paraguay *worked*, I assume the good things I do are *good enough*.

But when I look at my good deeds by a different standard—God's standard—I see that they are tattered and worn and stained. They are only filthy rags by His standard. Completely worthless. God is completely holy and perfect. Nothing that has not been perfected by Him can even be in His presence.

I realize now that nothing I can put on will work by this new standard. Nothing I do is good enough to gain me any merit in God's sight. Anything I try to do is only a filthy rag. His standard is absolute perfection, and no human—other than Jesus—has ever achieved that. That may seem like bad news but keep reading.

When we came to the States, we left behind a lot of our old clothing, and we obtained new attire. Spiritually, too, the only option I have to meet these new standards is to get rid of all my filthy rags and accept new clothing. My own stuff just won't do. It doesn't measure up. Thankfully, I am offered brand-new clothing through Jesus. Galatians

3:27 says, "For all of you who were baptized into Christ have clothed yourselves with Christ."

Because Christ was the only human who ever achieved perfection, He can offer me this new clothing—new life— called salvation. He alone can clothe me in the righteousness that God requires to enter His presence. Isaiah 61:10 says that He clothes us with the garment of salvation and wraps us in the robe of righteousness.

The minute we give up all the old, we are offered new clothing. When we put on these new garments of salvation, even our good deeds are forgiven and forgotten. Now God only sees our righteousness, and He allows us into His presence with a welcome smile and a big hug.

- -

On this earth I am still working on my wardrobe to make it fit the standards around me, but spiritually my wardrobe is complete. How about yours?

Have you received God's garment of salvation?

- -

I will rejoice greatly in the Lord, My soul will exult in my God; For He has clothed me with garments of salvation, He has wrapped me with a robe of righteousness.

Isaiah 61:10 (NASB95)

CHAPTER FIFTEEN

Fervent Prayers

I had been praying a lot. I couldn't help it. Someone was hurting, and I couldn't get her off my mind.

As God was slowly taking her earthly husband away from her over that week and a half, I prayed for both of them day and night. The flu visited our household, so some nights I was up almost every hour. While I was up, my mind turned to prayer for my hurting sister and brother in Christ. My prayers were vigilant, sometimes urgent, always fervent.

But as I was praying, I had a nagging sense of conviction.

So often my most fervent prayers are for the hurting saints. Compassion makes my heart go out to them. My heart hurts with them, and sometimes my eyes cry for them. Some of those saints are poised for their final takeoff—to be with their Creator in heaven forever.

But how often are my fervent prayers for those who are not yet saints? Does my heart hurt for them or my eyes cry for them? They are poised for eternal destruction, separated from their Creator forever.

Why do I find it easier to pray fervent prayers for a brother or sister in Christ—even if it is a prayer that they will tarry from entering a place of eternal joy and peace? And why do I neglect to pray for people who don't yet know God—even if it is prayers that they will be saved from falling to a place of eternal sadness and anguish? Proverbs 24:11 implores us to rescue those being led away to death and to hold back those who are staggering toward slaughter.

So, I set a challenge for myself.

Every time I pray for one of my brothers or sisters in Christ—for their earthly comfort, or even their tarrying from their eternal comfort—I want to pray for someone who is not yet a brother or sister in Christ. I want to pray that they will find this earthly comfort we pray for, and that they will become part of this family who knows how to pray for one another.

- -

Whom do you know that is being led away to
eternal death?

Will you join me in praying for our spiritual
family to grow?

- -

*Rescue those being led away to death; hold
back those staggering toward slaughter.*

Proverbs 24:11

CHAPTER SIXTEEN

The Flight

We arrived at the airport three hours early to check in for our flight back to Paraguay, and the check-in agents behind the counter were relaxed and helpful. We avoided potential disaster by asking about checking our bags all the way through—which the airline wasn't going to do at first.

The next hurdle was the seating. For the long, overnight flight each of our seats had been assigned to a different row scattered from the front to the back of the plane. Because the flight was full, the check-in agents couldn't rearrange them. We weren't really worried though. After all, who wouldn't try to juggle seats so young children could sit with their parents for an overnight flight where anything could happen: kids might need their meat cut up, have a nosebleed, throw up, or spill a drink.

Well, apparently the flight attendants wouldn't.

Miss "I Could Not Care Less If Your Family Sits Together" and "Señor Snippy" didn't lift even a pinky finger to help us. In fact, a few other flight attendants joined in fussing at us for not sitting down so the plane could take off. But thanks to a few kind passengers (and a few reluctant ones), we made an announcement to a whole section of the plane and ended up with three seats together and two directly behind them.

Needless to say, we were not impressed with this airline.

The sharp contrast between this flight and the one we had just made on a different airline was obvious. On that trip, the head flight attendant had announced to the entire cabin that the plane was not taking off until someone offered to change seats so a family with small children could be together. We felt seen and valued.

But the bitter beginning to this long flight had a sweet ending.

One kind flight attendant approached me at the end of our flight and said, "I heard that you have a long layover in Brazil," as he set a plastic bag on my lap.

"Yes, eight hours," I said, with a sideways smile, wondering why he was putting his trash bag on my lap.

"Maybe you can use this," he replied.

I peeked inside and found sandwiches, peach cups, cookies, pretzels, and water. Wow! And use it we did. This thoughtful gift helped us avoid the one expensive food kiosk in our confined waiting area. We ate from that bag for lunch and supper during our long wait. And each time we opened it, we smiled at the kindness of that one flight attendant in the midst of all the other uncaring ones.

The whole experience made me reflect on how even our simple actions have great potential—either for harm or for blessing.

The snippy flight attendant, with only a few words, set a tone that created a negative atmosphere. The other flight attendant, by her lack of words or action, said loudly, "I don't care," and marred the name of the business she represented. But the kind flight attendant—by a simple act of giving us leftover food that probably would have been thrown away—still blesses our hearts and has been lauded many times over in the telling of this story. Luke 6:31 says, "Do to others as you would have them do to you," and that is what this man did.

This makes me more determined that my words, which can slip out so easily, and my actions—or lack of actions— don't mar the name of the One I represent.

It also challenges me to think of small ways I can bless others. Because small actions can become big blessings, especially when people are in an unpleasant place in life.

Speak kind words. Be a blessing in simple ways. Your actions or words might have far-reaching effects.

- -

Who around you needs a kind word or small blessing today?

How have your words or actions today reflected the One you represent?

- -

*Do to others as you would have
them do to you.*

Luke 6:31

CHAPTER SEVENTEEN

Piques

Our week-long stay in the capital, Asuncion—attending meetings and buying materials to outfit the bathroom in our new house—gave us a welcome reprieve from the *piques* that plague us in the countryside of Paraguay.

A pique is a burrowing flea. They live in places where there are dirty animals (and what animals aren't dirty?), especially in places the sun doesn't reach. These tiny creatures feed on living things, including people. When they find a suitable host, they burrow into the skin to make a cozy nest for laying eggs—so even more piques can be hatched into this world.

Since these bugs can't hop far, they usually find a cranny around a person's toes, commonly beside the toenail. Then, usually unnoticed by their host, they begin burrowing. If still undetected, they create a sac around themselves, then fill it with tiny eggs. Before long, the flesh around the critter begins to swell and protest as the sac grows larger. First it itches, then becomes sore.

Once discovered, you need a needle, a good light source, and courage to begin digging. At this point, it can be rather painful to dig the bug and its gelatinous mass out of your irritated skin. Sometimes the pique is deeply embedded, and it leaves an ugly open crater in your toe when extracted.

These annoying little creatures remind me of sin.

Sin can be found anywhere people are—especially where the *Son* doesn't shine. Like piques, it's easy for sin to creep in unnoticed in our lives. James 1:15 says that desire conceives and gives birth to sin. Only those who are spiritually aware catch it before it digs in. And once it digs in, it quickly multiplies. A little itch might give us a clue that the sin is there, but if we ignore this symptom, we are surely destined for pain.

Leaving the sin to multiply can cause more and more pain. James also talks about sin growing. But digging the sin out can also be painful. Like the needle for the pique, sin needs a sharp, two-edged sword and the Source of Light. Sometimes the sin is deeply embedded and extracting it can be difficult. If the sin has been left long, a nasty crater is sure to be a result of the extraction.

After removing the pique—or the sin—a healing salve and bandage will prevent infection or reinfestation.

Avoiding piques in Paraguay is a never-ending chore. In our household, it became a ritual during pique season to do a pique-check on all toes before going to bed. This way they could sometimes be caught before they dug in or could be quickly extracted if they had gotten a foothold.

Our lives need the same kind of daily sin-check.

If we make this a practice, we can quickly get rid of sin before it takes hold and makes a painful mess. Of course, not loitering in places where piques are propagated—where the sun doesn't shine—will help you avoid becoming a tempting host for them. And so it is with sin. If we don't put ourselves in places where sin sees us as a tasty host, we will be much better off.

Another way to repel piques is to habitually spray a disinfectant around your home. Spiritually, if we regularly wash ourselves with God's Word, we will repel sin. Just once won't work long, though. Those nasty critters will come crawling right back. The cleansing must be a regular habit.

A different way to keep piques away is to let the sun shine on them. They are creatures of darkness and love shady places. Sin, too, can be decimated by letting the Son shine on it. Sin loves to hide in shady places, but when we expose it to the truth of God's light, it will flee. First John 1:7 says that if we walk in the light, as He is in the light, the blood of Jesus purifies us from all sin.

Pay attention to small itches and pains that need to be dealt with in your life. Be meticulous about your own pique-check. Avoid plaguing places. Wash regularly with God's Word. And let the *Son* shine in!

- -

In what shady places in your life could sin go unnoticed?

What itches might you be ignoring?

- -

But if we walk in the light, as he is in the light, we have fellowship with one another, and the blood of Jesus, his Son, purifies us from all sin.

1 John 1:7

CHAPTER EIGHTEEN

Hidden Blessings

After returning to Paraguay from home assignment, my husband was working hard on fixing up the house we would live in once we moved to our new town—about forty-five bumpy minutes from the rural town where we currently lived. That meant I was home with the kids—without him and without a car for a few weeks.

We had sold our motorcycle before our home assignment in the States and hadn't yet bought another, so I didn't even have that as a means of transportation. I was using "bus line 11"—also known as my own two legs.

I love the way God hides little blessings in what we might be tempted to see as inconveniences. Isaiah 45:3 says that God gives us hidden treasures in secret places.

In addition to homeschooling, my youngest son went to Paraguayan kindergarten every day to learn the language and culture (the other boys would start their grade in the Paraguayan school when we moved). Instead of whisking him from the lunch table to the motorcycle to his school in just a few minutes, we had to leave fifteen minutes earlier to walk the kilometer together. But while we walked, we shared mommy and son time—for a whole blissful fifteen minutes. A hidden treasure.

As we walked, we talked.

Many times, we practiced Spanish and Guarani words that he might hear in school since he still didn't understand much yet. Sometimes I went into the schoolyard with him and chatted with the teachers before school started. Then I headed back down the dusty, dirt road for another blissful fifteen minutes—just me and God in that secret place.

With an occasional wave and *adios* when passing someone on the road, I prayed for my son, back at school. I prayed for my husband and the guys working on the house. And I prayed for whatever else came to mind in those peaceful moments of reprieve from the daily busyness.

Life in Paraguay isn't as hectic and hurried as in the States, but it is nonetheless busy and chock-full. We don't have all the conveniences that make things faster in the US. No dishwasher, no dryer, no microwave, no drive-throughs. All those tasks still need to be done—but by hand.

With homeschooling three grades, cooking everything from scratch, hanging out laundry, and cleaning the unbelievable piles of dirt, my day was full from dawn till dusk. For a while, I had someone to come and help with the cleaning and laundry. But since our family was just "camping out" while preparing to move, I hadn't asked anyone to help.

But again—hidden blessings.

The kids pitched in and worked as a team to get the daily tasks done so our family had time to relax and enjoy other activities. My eleven-year-old went three times a week—on his bike or line 11—to get milk from our friend who was up at 4:30 a.m. to milk her cows. Thankfully, my husband usually did the pasteurizing and separated the cream.

Many times, all three boys were at the sink—washing, rinsing, and drying the dishes—while I read aloud from homeschool books. They learned where everything in the kitchen went so they could easily hand me things for cooking or put dishes away themselves.

They also learned the fine art of hanging clothes on the line—or racing to grab them off when a rainstorm came. That's something most boys their age are clueless about.

They also helped juice oranges, clean the bathroom, feed the animals, burn the trash, dump the compost, and sweep the porch. I dare say all that extra work—which they may not have considered a blessing at all—was building character in them that will serve them well for the rest of their lives.

Our God is so big and so loving that He makes even things that don't *seem* like blessings work together for some good. And He delights in giving good things.

- -

What hidden blessings might be in your
empty places?

- -

*I will give you hidden treasures, riches stored in
secret places so that you may know that
I am the* LORD.

Isaiah 45:3

CHAPTER NINETEEN

Leaving Paradise

T ony and I sat on the porch sipping our hot coffee, enjoying the cool morning rain.

In front of us, draping daintily from the edge of the roof and framing our view to the yard, was a bougainvillea vine, each branch dangling with a spray of fuchsia-colored flowers. Just beyond that was the grape arbor, heavy with this year's bumper crop of still-green grapes. Each tight cluster dripped with the smell of cool rain. The fence on the far side of the arbor was covered with grapevines, too, forming an almost complete wall of dripping, mottled leaves.

Growing up one post of the arbor was a vine dotted with delicate, lantern-shaped, white flowers—each tipped with a tiny red tongue. Another post was circled by ferns and orchids. In the backyard, our big, white porch swing hung between two majestic *oveña* trees. The trunks of those trees were adorned with lush vines, thick ivies, and clusters of orchids.

Beside them was the peach tree we planted years ago, hanging with the best peaches we had ever seen on a tree in Paraguay. Nearby were the blackberry vines along the back fence, the first berries just about to turn black and sweet. In the garden beyond the oveñas were many banana plants as well as raspberry bushes that had already given us pints of tart, ruby-red jam.

Looking at this view made us smile and sigh with contentment.

Our home in San Francisco, Paraguay, was a comfortable and happy place to live. We worked for years helping it to become this Edenic scene. My husband designed the house, and it was built by skilled workers. This was our homestead—strong, stable, convenient, and well-constructed.

There we raised many sheep, chickens, ducks, turkeys, and rabbits—not to mention our three boys. We entertained guests, made family memories, and hosted Bible studies, youth meetings, prayer meetings, Sunday morning church, birthday parties, and Thanksgiving feasts. In that house and in that town, we built fourteen years' worth of satisfying relationships.

But now we were leaving.

One part of my heart constricted and wanted to hang on. Those fourteen years had been a dream come true. Sure, there had been highs and lows, tears and laughter. But the life and ministry we had there—and the relationships we built—had been fun, fulfilling, and even exhilarating.

Yet the other part of my heart beat for what was still out there.

So many people still needed to hear how to have a satisfying and life-changing relationship with a God who loves them more than they can ever imagine.

So, Christ's love compelled us—to leave all that behind and move on to another town that had no gospel witness.

When I thought of the paradise Jesus left behind in heaven to come to this earth so we could experience His love, my utopia that I was tempted to cling to faded in comparison. Philippians 2:5–8 talks about this. Jesus humbled Himself to come and be our servant. How could I not be willing to leave behind my wilted shadow of a paradise in order to tell others about this abundant love they can experience?

If Jesus can leave the perfection of heaven—and be separated from His Father through a cruel death at the hands of the very ones He came to save—then I, too, could leave behind what I had grown to love dearly.

Like Jesus, Tony and I did it intentionally, gladly, and whole-heartedly.

For the potential of what lay ahead, we moved on.

- -

What beautiful things are you holding on to
that God might want you to let go of for the
potential of what lies ahead?

- -

*Christ Jesus: Who, being in very nature God,
did not consider equality with God something
to be used to his own advantage; rather, he
made himself nothing by taking the very nature
of a servant, being made in human likeness.
And being found in appearance as a man, he
humbled himself by becoming obedient to
death—even death on a cross!*

Philippians 2:5–8

CHAPTER TWENTY

Go Crazy, Daddy!

"Go crazy, Daddy! Go crazy!"

When I was a child, my sisters and I often said that to our daddy when he was driving. Our family had a 1969 Plymouth Barracuda, and we girls loved riding in the back of it. Before seatbelt laws, we sometimes sat in the hatchback and hung onto a metal bar that went across the back of the back seat. Then in conniving, gleeful unison we said those words:

"Go crazy, Daddy! Go crazy!"

If the conditions were right, then Daddy obliged us by gently swerving one way, then the other. With delighted squeals, we, too, leaned exaggeratedly one way then the other with the curves, hanging onto that bar. We leaned heavily on one another, and sometimes the sister on the end toppled over with elated laughter.

Then we giddily said, "Do it again, Daddy! Do it again!"

Without fail, we saw our daddy's smiling eyes in the rearview mirror. He loved making his daughters laugh, and we loved the thrill he gave us by "going crazy."

That is how Tony and I felt about our heavenly Father and the delightful things He was doing in planting His church in Paraguay as we left the first church plant and started again. He had let us sit in a fun back seat while He drove this great adventure called life. We hung on tight and yelled, "Go crazy, Daddy! Go crazy!" And He did His thing! He created a church where there wasn't one before.

First, He gently swerved one way and touched a heart, then swerved the other way and another person fell head over heels in love with Him. What a thrill! We hung on in exhilaration as we watched Him drive, and we leaned into the curves with all our strength while we egged Him on with delight, saying again and again, "Go crazy, Daddy! Go crazy!"

I'm sure He was smiling back at us and enjoying us as we enjoyed Him and His incredible adventures. We love the thrill He gave us those fourteen years in church planting in San Francisco, Paraguay. And as we started again in a new town, our hearts cried out, "Do it again, Daddy! Do it again!"

The prophet Habakkuk understood this kind of longing when he said in Habakkuk 3:1–2, "I stand in awe of your deeds, Lord. Repeat them in our day." We definitely stand in awe of what God has done in Paraguay, and we want to see Him do it over and over again!

- -

Where have you seen God work in your life?

Where did He "go crazy"?

Where do you want to see Him do it again?

- -

LORD, I have heard of your fame;
I stand in awe of your deeds, LORD.
Repeat them in our day,
in our time make them known.

Habakkuk 3:2

CHAPTER TWENTY-ONE

I Was Thankful

The inside walls of my new house reminded me of a medieval prison. They were unfinished concrete etched with wavy scratch marks. The floor was the same—rough concrete that wore away with normal use, creating impressive piles of sand when I swept. And when I swept, great clouds of dust rose and settled like smog over the contents of the room.

But I was grateful.

The parts of my house that were not so nice reminded me to be grateful for the things that were—and to count my blessings.

The furniture stood in stark contrast to the shell of the house. It seemed misplaced against those prison-like walls. A beautiful three-foot-square table Tony made from Paraguayan hardwood stood in the tiny living room/dining room/guest room combo. It folded out into a six-foot table for guests, practically spanning the whole room.

Two majestic lawyer (barrister) bookcases, each shelf enclosed behind a glass door, were filled with books—books that would cost a Paraguayan two lifetimes of wages—if they were even available there. Beside them was Tony's masterpiece: a sturdy mission-style rocking chair—the most comfortable seat in the house—maybe even in all of Paraguay.

We also had a couch with a trundle bed, making it a versatile double bed or two singles. Many Paraguayans sleep several kids to a bed. What adaptable luxury I had to offer my guests.

From the living room, I looked through an open window into the kitchen and saw another of Tony's masterpieces: the kitchen cabinets. They were made of beautiful Paraguayan redwood and featured a white contrast on the doors. The kitchen countertops were forest-green faux marble Formica.

But bits of that rough prison wall showed between the upper and lower cabinets, reminding me again to be grateful. Most of my neighbors had no cabinets at all—only a few rough, wooden shelves. The beautiful counters and the cabinets were like jewels to me, and I was grateful I had running water in my kitchen. Having a gas stove instead of a cooking fire and having a refrigerator and even a small chest freezer was over-the-top luxury in Paraguay.

The two bedrooms of the house had smooth stucco walls, so we were able to paint them. But reminders to be thankful remained. Sometimes I had to tug and twist, then finally yank the useless latch completely out of the window just to open the bifold glass panes. And they swung inward so no furniture could be near them. But then I reminded myself: What a blessing to have glass windows at all! Wooden shutters—what most people in Paraguay have—can only be either open to let in light (as well as cold, heat, or rain), or closed to keep out heat, cold, rain, or bugs but then deprive you of light.

The big, junky-looking loft shelf running along the top of each bedroom was far from convenient. But it reminded me to be grateful for the treasures stored there: thick blankets for the winter; extra sheets, towels, and pillows for us and our guests; seasonal decorations; suitcases for travel to Asuncion or the States; and even toys the kids weren't using.

Like the dark places of a painting make the light places stand out, the ugliness, inconvenience, or annoyances in my house only made the beauty and comfort shine brighter. And they reminded me to be grateful.

Those negative parts of my physical environment whispered to me—a phrase I often heard my grandma say—"This world is not my home."

When I was tempted to roll my eyes at the ugliness or be frustrated with the inconveniences, I remembered that beauty and convenience are not why Tony and I are here. Second Corinthians 4:18 tells me that beauty and convenience are only temporary. Beauty and convenience are bonuses. Most people around me had little of either. The ugliness was a reminder to go out of my house—out to my neighbors, who lived with much less than I had.

That is why I was here.

The people around me had neither such temporal beauty and comforts in their physical environment nor the eternal beauty of a spiritual relationship with their Creator. The beauty and comforts here on this earth, or even the lack of them, are negligible in the light of eternity. And eternity is what this life allows us to get ready for.

I want to use this life—full of its inconveniences and ugliness but also sprinkled with beauty and convenience—to point as many as possible to my Father's eternal house that will have beauty and comforts beyond our wildest imagination.

- -

What comforts do you need to be grateful for?

How can the difficult or ugly things in your life remind you to focus on what is unseen and eternal?

- -

For our light and momentary troubles are achieving for us an eternal glory that far outweighs them all. So we fix our eyes not on what is seen, but on what is unseen, since what is seen is temporary, but what is unseen is eternal.

2 Corinthians 4:17–18

CHAPTER TWENTY-TWO
Discrepancies

Sometime after realizing that the inconvenient and ugly things in my house could help me focus on the good and the eternal, Tony and I upgraded a bit of the ugly. For Mother's Day he put up a beautiful tile backsplash in our kitchen.

Back when we were buying tile to make a bathroom in this yet unfinished house, I found some delightful purple and green tiles and immediately thought they would be perfect for a kitchen backsplash someday.

When we found this house to rent in the tiny, rural town we felt God calling us to, we were delighted. The house was strong and well-built—but unfinished. All we had to work with was rough cement walls and floors, a shell with only a dirt floor where the bathroom should be, and a tiny, dark cell for a kitchen.

With his gifts and abilities, Tony transformed that kitchen into a bright, bay-windowed haven. The bathroom took shape from a formless void into a useful room. The owner let us use these improvements as rent, but much of the house we left unfinished to avoid investing years of rent up front.

So, I lived in a house of contrasting ambiance.

As I looked at my kitchen, I saw the beautiful wood and white cabinets with the green countertops, and now the beautiful white tile backsplash—scattered with those quaint purple and green tiles. The grapes on the curtains and the green tile floor drew it all together. It was comfortable and homey.

But the comfy, clean kitchen stood in stark contrast to the next room.

The beautiful, easy-to-clean tile floor changed abruptly in the living room/dining area to that brittle cement that turned to sand when I swept. The unfinished walls had long drip marks under the window where rain seeped in and stained the wall as it ran toward the floor.

As I sat at the handsome table Tony built and had my quiet time in the early morning light, I saw both rooms at once through the window-like opening between them. On one side, unfinished cement. On the other, the quaint, cozy kitchen.

And somewhere deep inside me I loved the discrepancy.

The drab, gray walls reminded me of my neighbors— not only their homes, which are often far more humble than mine—but their hearts. Most don't know Jesus yet. Their lives are unfinished too—gray and lacking.

The kitchen represented my comfort zone. My haven. There I happily worked to give sustenance to my family and bake a myriad of delicacies to add flare to life. But when my eyes shifted back to the bare concrete, I was reminded: *a world beyond my comfort zone* desperately needs Jesus.

That world called to me. It desired more. It needed more. No flares or delicacies existed there, just mundane survival in lives that were as incomplete as my walls. This severe discrepancy in front of me was a constant reminder to go out of my comfort zone and into the world of my neighbors because I know the One who can finish those lives and decorate them with color and happiness. This incongruity called me out to tell them what, or rather Who, will complete them and make their world come alive with delicacies that they could never even imagine. Christ's love compelled me, like 2 Corinthians 5 says, to go to them and tell them about His love.

Let's leave our comfortable kitchen occasionally to help others who lack not only physical but spiritual luxuries. There is a world out there begging to be completed. Let's make it beautiful with God's transforming love.

. . . .

What is your comfortable kitchen?

What prevents you from stepping out of it?

Who needs to hear about God's finishing work?

. . . .

For Christ's love compels us.

2 Corinthians 5:14

CHAPTER TWENTY-THREE

Blessings in the Barrenness

As we walked along the concrete path on our home assignment—beside the serene stream, drinking in the beauty of fall (which we never have in Paraguay)—I couldn't help myself.

Every once in a while, I had to scoop up some dead leaves from the ground, hold them up to my nose, and take a deep breath.

Ahh.

The earthy, nostalgic smell of oak leaves brought a smile to my face.

Autumn could be seen as a sad time. The leaves fall off the trees, leaving them bare and ugly. But without autumn, there would be no stately, brilliant change of colors, no leaves shimmering to the ground, no pungent, earthy smell of barrenness.

Such beauty. Such blessing.

All the barren moments we've experienced in Paraguay came to mind.

The unbearable heat that turns you into a sluggish lizard.

The times when the electricity was off too—so not even a fan stirred the air.

The moments we prayed for rain—a temporary reprieve from the heat.

The days we had no running water—sometimes for days at a time—so we went to the neighbor's well for a bucket of water to bathe.

The tarantulas we found in the shower.

And days of winter when the cold crept so deeply into our bones that we couldn't imagine having ever been warm.

Those physical difficulties were undoubtedly oppressive. They take precedence when they are present. But even deeper was emotional barrenness—the absence of people we love, especially when important or difficult things happen in our lives or theirs. The lack of parents or siblings nearby when important things are on your mind is a difficult void to fill.

But all of it—all those moments—were included in the gratitude I felt in that deeply inhaled breath of earthiness.

The difficult things in life are the shaded areas in a beautiful picture. They give contrast and bring out the light. They give depth and beauty to the overall picture.

Because I've experienced the heat, I'm giddy with excitement to live in a house with air-conditioning on home assignment. What luxury.

Because I've taken bucket baths, I delight in a real shower inside my house—and *two* of them—over-the-top lavishness.

Because of tarantulas, swarms of mosquitoes, and armies of ants, I'm grateful for good windows and doors. What affluence.

Because of the cold, I praise God for warmth at the touch of a button. Sheer opulence.

And because I've experienced the deep void of family who are far away, every drop of coffee sipped together is liquid gold, and every word exchanged a precious diamond.

I could go on and on—muddy roads, difficult language—but *all* those difficulties are included within the circle of blessing.

Not only because they have passed and I have the comforts once again. I am also grateful for the blessing *in* them that I would have missed otherwise.

I understand my neighbors in Paraguay better because I experience the same difficulties. When there is no water, I go to my neighbor's well. She gets to be the hero. We experience the hard time together.

The extreme heat forces us to the shade of a mango tree. There we drink the typical cold tea shared with friends. The conversation is about real life and real things and sometimes leads us to talk about God.

When it's cold, our family huddles around the little wood stove for breakfast or snuggles under the covers to read a book. Childhood memories are made from these moments.

When family members are far away, we run to our heavenly Father and talk to Him instead.

Let's do what 1 Thessalonians 5:18 says and thank God together for our many blessings—*and* for the blessing of barrenness.

. . . .

What difficult things can you thank God for?

What good things have your barren places created for you?

. . . .

In everything give thanks; for this is God's will for you in Christ Jesus.

1 Thessalonians 5:18 (NASB95)

CHAPTER TWENTY-FOUR

Don't Get Too Comfortable

More than half of our home assignment in the States had flown by, and we were looking at cramming in all the things we wanted to accomplish and experience. We were thinking about how to finish well.

As we began to wind things up, I found myself thinking, "No, don't buy another one of those—just use up what you have, then make do until we get back to Paraguay." In the back of my mind there was a voice that said, "Don't get too comfortable here."

Home assignment is a special time, but it has its strange parts. We finally get to be with family and friends, reconnect, and make memories together—but we know that it is only for a time. We dig deeply into this different country for a year, but we don't want to get too comfortable because we know we must leave again.

Getting comfortable could be so easy here.

There are two bathrooms in our house.

Central heat and air.

Drive-through restaurants, sit-down restaurants, shiny cars, smooth roads.

A dishwasher, a dryer.

Stores galore for anything you need—or just want.

But comfort is not why we came to the States.

Granted, a reprieve from the discomforts of life on the field is a huge bonus. As we share stories about Paraguay during our times in the States, inevitably tales of discomfort come up—unbearable heat, deplorable cold, unimaginable piles of dirt and dishes, difficult language or culture moments, stuck-in-the-mud stories, ants, snakes, spiders, no internet, no electricity, and/or no water.

Stories like these may make people wonder:

Why would you go back to Paraguay?

Tempting as it is, getting comfortable here is not our calling. There is something more that calls us back to Paraguay. The love of Christ compels us to go back to our Paraguayan friends—to tell them about the transforming relationship they can have with God.

So, we know we must leave again.

As believers, none of us should get too comfortable, because this world—this life—is not our last stop. We should make the most of every opportunity, and as Thoreau put it, "Suck all the marrow out of life." But as

Jesus said, we should also "not store up for ourselves treasures on earth where moth and rust destroy."

We, too, are leaving.

This world is not our home. There is more.

That is what we should be preparing for—and living for. Our true investments are the ones that last for eternity.

Let us live life intentionally.

Let's praise God for the comforts we have, while also intentionally pushing ourselves outside our comfort zone so we can make investments in people's lives that we and they can take with them.

Jesus did that.

He lived life to its fullest while on this earth, but He knew that this was not the end. He didn't get too comfortable. He had His eyes on the goal, which is eternity.

He traded the comforts of this world for the cross—to pay for our sins so we could have eternal comforts.

One day we will breathe that sigh of relief and know we can finally get comfortable.

Because we'll be in that perfect home.

There the comforts will be beyond what we even dared to dream of here.

But until then, let's not get too comfortable in this life.

- -

What comforts might God be calling you to leave in order to tell others about Him?

- -

Do not store up for yourselves treasures on earth, where moth and rust destroy, and where thieves break in and steal. But store up for yourselves treasures in heaven where neither moth nor rust destroys, and where thieves do not break in and steal.

Matthew 6:19–20 (NASB95)

CHAPTER TWENTY-FIVE

The Out-of-Place Crystal

One Christmas was a special one for Tony and me because we spent it in the States with our family. Among the gifts I received was a beautiful Swarovski crystal snowflake. It is a special treasure to me because, growing up, my mother always had little crystal figures in our kitchen window.

One of my childhood memories is of quiet mornings with warm sunshine filtering through the kitchen window into the room filled with wonderful breakfast smells and magical rainbow colors sprinkled cheerfully all over the kitchen walls. I was delighted to have a crystal of my own.

Naturally, this was one of the treasures that made the cut to be taken back to Paraguay.

I was delighted when we unwrapped it again and hung it in my kitchen window. Sure enough, it sprinkled cheerful rainbows on the wall of my kitchen too.

The next Christmas when I got out the decorations, there was a dollar-store window cling nativity scene. My kitchen window had the biggest pane of glass in our house, so it naturally went there.

The snowflake was already hanging there, so I positioned the nativity scene around it—and it became the star above the manger. I giggled as I stepped back. It seemed clever.

As the days passed, something about the scene was unsettling. Something was amiss—like a small splinter, constantly irritating.

That beautiful Swarovski crystal hanging beside the dollar-store window clings. It just didn't fit. The donkey's ear was disintegrating from the heat and humidity. The wise man's head was half torn off. The roof of the stable tore right in two when I took it off the plastic backing. I just stuck it back together—right over the manger and Joseph and Mary.

And the window. It was so dirty. Right above the sink where we washed an endless stream of dishes after cooking everything from scratch, it was constantly spattered with crud.

Even the beautiful rainbows of light seemed strangely out of place. The bay window of my kitchen was a beautiful place to look out on the lush green of the grape harbor right outside and the quaint garden of flowers beyond it. But the light coming through the window cast the bright rainbows right onto the unfinished, rough, gray cement wall on the other side of the kitchen. They seemed so out of place there.

But the longer I pondered the scene, the more fitting this seemingly mismatched scene was.

It fit right in with Advent. Wasn't Jesus just like this Swarovski crystal surrounded by cheap window clings? Like Philippians 2:6-7 says, He did not consider His majestic equality with God something to hang on to; but gave up everything to become a servant to us humans.

He was a precious jewel beyond the world's imagination, yet there He was lying in the place where cows eat.

We've had a cow. We've seen a manger. It is not where I would want to lay my baby.

And yet ...

There He was.

God Himself.

The Light of the universe—right here in this rough, gray world.

He came right into the uncomfortable heat and humidity—where people's lives are torn and battered and nothing is perfect. Was the beam of His stable even patched together like my window cling?

He came right into the daily stream of our messy lives spattered with crud, and He did it on purpose.

That is amazing.

He did it for a very special purpose. He came into this dirty, torn world so we can be with Him forever in eternity.

I wonder if, while on this earth, He kept looking back to the beauty of heaven to remind Himself of what He was here for. Then He kept lovingly casting His beautiful light onto our unfinished lives.

He was out of place in this world.

But oh, for what a wonderful reason!

We are grateful that we, too, can be "out of place" in Paraguay—reflecting God's beautiful light into a dark place where people desperately need to see how they can have a life-changing relationship and a perfect home with Him forever.

- -

Where might God be calling you to be "out of place" so you can shine His light into dark places?

- -

Christ Jesus: who, being in very nature God, did not consider equality with God something to be used to his own advantage; rather, he made himself nothing by taking the very nature of a servant, being made in human likeness. And being found in appearance as a man, he humbled himself by becoming obedient to death—even death on a cross!

Philippians 2:5–8

CHAPTER TWENTY-SIX

The Forest, the Dance

W e truly enjoyed living in the mountains of Tennessee for our year of home assignment. Almost every morning Tony and I got to look at the sunrise over the Appalachian Mountains. After the kids headed off to school, we often sat on our back deck and looked out over the beautiful woods behind our home.

The leaves of each tree were constantly in motion. As a whole, the forest shimmered in the dappled morning light. The movement of the leaves caused individual ones to suddenly reflect the golden light—flashing as they twisted and turned.

When I focused on one tree, each branch gently swayed to its own rhythm, slightly different from every other branch. Each leaf also had its own movement, the gentle wind hitting it at a unique angle. Some leaves did a wild, joyful dance out front, reflecting that dappled light in ecstatic praise to God. Others gently bobbed or weaved following the current at the moment.

Even leaves in the shadows were faintly moving. But their gentle motion added depth to the whole beautiful picture. The entire forest became a complex, beautiful dance of individual movements blending into one breathtaking whole.

I have always loved trees, and as I gazed at them, I was struck by how much a forest resembles the Body of Christ. 1 Corinthians 12:12 says, "Just as a body, though one, has many parts, but all its many parts form one body, so it is with Christ."

The Body of Christ is made up of so many individuals and groups—each moved by the wind of God in unique ways, depending on their position, situation, and season. Some individuals are out front, reflecting God brightly and enthusiastically—waving God's praise in front of a watching world. They attract attention and show that something bigger is moving and illuminating them.

Some churches—like branches—are moving more vigorously, the whole branch responding in unison to God's wind. Within that branch each member—or leaf—has its personal dance, twisting and turning yet still bobbing with the branch.

Other branches in the shadows move delicately in their own motion—no less blown by the gentle breeze of God. They add depth and peace to the bigger picture.

Some individual leaves are behind others and receive the gentlest of breezes, moving quietly. Yet they, too, are part of that never-ceasing, multifaceted dance.

Each limb, each branch, each leaf—

All unique,

    All essential,

        All part of the sacred, diverse forest.

Let's cherish every movement, every dance, every subtle sway.

And may we see the whole forest—the Body of Christ—as the magnificent masterpiece it is.

- -

How is the wind of God moving in your life right now?

What value do you find in other parts of the larger Body?

- -

Just as a body, though one, has many parts, but all its many parts form one body, so it is with Christ.

1 Corinthians 12:12

CHAPTER TWENTY-SEVEN

A New Name

One of the things we were hoping for—before we even returned to Paraguay after home assignment—was to have another parakeet.

In years past, we had enjoyed raising one from a chick. We fed it mashed bananas, and it got used to being handled. When we gathered outside for *terere* (the communal Paraguayan cold tea) it sat on our shoulders or nibbled on our ears—even imitated human sounds. Sadly, that parakeet died just before our family left for the US.

When we returned, we went to the market in search of a baby parakeet, but we were disappointed to find only a grown one for sale. Typically, mature birds caught in the wild are not ideal. They're noisy, aggressive, and hard to tame.

But to our delight, this bird was actually both tame and quiet.

The first thing it did, however, was chew its way out of the cardboard box we had brought it home in. Hence its name: Houdini.

After a quick but frantic chase around the room, we realized how tame he was. His clingy feet walked all over us. He snuggled his soft green and blue feathers in our hands and perched on our shoulders. He was more than we had expected—a perfect gift from God.

We cleaned up the cage we had used before, gave him water, seeds, and even a peeled banana. He had all he needed. Satisfied, I left him on the porch and went to water the newly planted garden before dark.

But when I returned, the cage was empty.

The small door was still closed and secured with a wire, just like I'd left it. Houdini had lived up to his name! We realized sadly that he must be smaller than our last bird—and had gone right through the bars at the top.

We were devastated.

It was dusk and getting darker by the minute. We frantically grabbed headlamps and flashlights and searched for Houdini in all the places he could hide. But he was exactly the same color as the plants and leaves of the trees. We combed the flowers, plants, hedges, and trees, the garden, even the duck and chicken pen.

Nothing.

The more the minutes ticked by, the less chance of finding him again. Finally, it was just too dark. It seemed impossible.

We went to bed thinking of Houdini out in the big world alone. His clipped wing meant he couldn't fly far or defend himself from predators. We dolefully prayed that God might protect him and bring him back.

The next morning, we resumed our search in spurts as we had time—first with hope, then as the day went on with limp sadness. We each sent up our silent and solitary prayers and went to bed with melancholy hearts. Why would God give us such a perfect gift, only to take it away again?

Another day passed. Every bird tweet sparked momentary hope. But each chirp was also a reminder of how impossible Houdini's return seemed.

On the third day, while I was outside drinking terere, a little girl came to the gate.

"Did you lose a parakeet?" she asked.

"Yes," I replied curiously.

"Would you pay me to bring it back to you?" she replied.

Annoyed, but smiling, I said, "Sure, I will pay you."

I had already planned to buy another one but would much rather have Houdini back.

She explained that she had found a parakeet at her house the day before and had told our common neighbor, to whom I had told our story.

I followed her home, carrying a cage with smaller bars. She led me into her dirt-floored, board and batten kitchen, where she and her mother cooked over a fire. The girl lifted a wooden board from a five-gallon bucket and scooped out Houdini.

I gave her some money and thanked her. She seemed satisfied.

"This bird is like us," I said, as her eyebrows lifted ever so slightly and her eyes searched for more information.

"God made us and gave us everything we need, but we weren't satisfied—we wandered away. He longed for a relationship with us—yet we ran further. Still, He protected us—despite the dangers we didn't even know were there."

She listened carefully, maybe hearing this for the first time. It was one drop in her understanding of the gospel message.

Now Houdini has a new name: Ransom.

We bought him back—just like God bought us back.

God ransomed us. He paid the price for us running away from Him—even though He was the one who gave us all we needed in the first place. He, too, gives us a new name. Revelation 2:17 says "To the one who is victorious … I will also give that person a white stone with a new name written on it."

We put ourselves in grave danger when we wandered away from Him—more than we ever knew. Yet He protected us even while we ran away from Him. He wanted a relationship with us and was sad when we left.

God gets enjoyment from our existence.

Just like my family and I now delight in our bird named Ransom.

- -

Do you run from God's care for you?

What good things is He offering that you are shunning?

- -

To the one who is victorious ... I will also give that person a white stone with a new name written on it.

Revelation 2:17